Table of Content

Michela Fantinel, the Author of The Utimate Guide to Australia Itineraries

Copyright ©2014 to-present date by Michela Fantinel

Disclaimer

This book reflects the author's personal experiences and provides helpful tips. Each reader is advised to complete detailed research to confirm the suitability of the information contained in this book. We disclaim any liability or responsibility for the accuracy of the information contained in this book as well as any injury, loss, damage and inconvenience arising by any reader using the information contained in this book.

Note About this Paperback Edition

Hi,

I'm Michela, thanks for purchasing my book!

Please note that inside the book you will come across destinations and resources where a short link to a website or a blog post may display. You can copy it onto the browser of your computer or phone to be able to access those webpages.

However, to make things easier for you, I'll be happy to send you the digital format of the "**Travel Resources Section**" of this book.

Thus you can use these resources for planning your trip to Australia.

This is my bonus that you get for FREE.

To claim your bonus and free copy of the travel resources guide, please send an email to info@rockytravel.net and I will email you the PDF file.

Feel free to get in touch with me via email if you have any questions to: info@rockytravel.net

Happy Reading and Planning!

Michela Fantinel

Why this Australia Travel Book?

In over 14 years of travels I've criss-crossed Australia from bottom to top and west to east. I've travelled by car, train, plane, and group tour. I know how important it is to be well-prepared and have everything in place before travelling.

A well thought out itinerary allows you to see Australia without having to make changes last minute. This means you'll maximize your time and potentially save up to 1500 Australian dollars on your budget.

Not to mention it gives you the peace of mind you need to immerse yourself in the Australian lifestyle. You'll be able to get close to the locals, savour their cultural traditions, and learn about the real Australia. By allocating the right time to each place, you'll be able to travel stress-free and make memories to last a lifetime.

I wrote this book from my "*solo female traveller point of view*"; however, everything contained in this book can be adjusted whether you're travelling alone or with a companion.

The first part focuses on the **how-to**, thus saving you hours of wading through the abundance of information on the internet. It gives you the in-depth knowledge you need to quickly identify the right itinerary for you. The second part outlines four step-by-step itineraries around Australia.

As a first time solo traveller to Australia, you want to see as much as you can. You can't afford to make mistakes, choose the wrong activities, or miss out on things you would have loved to see.

The hardest part about creating a good itinerary in Australia is balancing your time frame with the places you want to see and the distances you have to travel.

This book will guide you through all the steps. It shows you how much time you need for each place, what you can and can't do, and how to maximize your time and make cost-effective choices.

Why travel Australia? The first steps...

Consider these steps when you start to make your itinerary:

- **Set a time frame:** And stick to it. You'll also want to set a focus for your trip. Do you want to see nature or cities? Outback or beaches?

- **Make a list of must-dos and must-sees**: Then make sure they're a good match with the time of year you're planning to visit.

- **Draw a rough plan**: Once you do this, calculate the distances to see if it's viable. You'll probably have to eliminate several spots to get a maximum of four or five destinations. (There's always next time!)

- **Consider all transportation methods**: Choose the most cost-effective ones that also allow you to maximize your time.

- **Fix a budget**: You'll need this to stay on track.

- **Make 80% of arrangements**: But leave 10-20% to be decided upon spontaneously.

When crafting your itinerary, build it at your own pace and always emphasize slow travel. Choose self-driving routes that match your level of experience. Be realistic, and make sure the distances work with your schedule.

Why is good Trip Planning vital? Because...

- **You can't afford to make changes to your plan last minute**: This will increase the cost of your trip by 100-200%. In Australia, distances are huge; it takes a long time to move from A to B. Cheap flights and internal transportation must be booked in advance to save 30-50% on normal rates.

- **You can't waste time doing extra research when in Australia**: You're there to discover places and experience a new country, not to plan and revise your itinerary. The vast majority of your planning must be completed before leaving for Australia.

Though we'll delve into the details later on in the book, you should ask yourself these questions before you do anything else.

They'll help you get a rough idea of what you want your trip to look like, which will help you when we discuss more detailed planning in a little bit.

1. What's my focus?

Like any good blueprint, your trip needs a focus, a goal, a purpose. With a clear focus, it's easier to identify areas and destinations to include in your itinerary.

What's your plan? Do you want to go on road trips? Learn to surf? Hike in national parks? Watch wildlife? Or maybe you prefer indulging in food and wine tastings?

Do you love to travel in style at a relaxed pace and stay in luxury hotels; or do you prefer to camp and be active in the great outdoors?

Once you figure out your desired activities and travel style, the rest of your itinerary will be easy to plan. Australia offers a wealth of activities and unique experiences. What you need to know is how to match your time frame to places and activities.

Here are some more questions you need to ask...

2. When should I visit Australia?

The time of year you visit plays an important role in your choice of itineraries. We'll discuss this in further detail later, but here's some basic information.

While northern tropical regions of Australia are better for winter months (May-September), the rest of Australia is best from spring to autumn (October-March). That being said, some destinations in spring and summer tend to be crowded.

Make a list of the places you want to see, along with the time frame you have set, and then go through and whittle it down to a maximum of four to five destinations on a 20-30 day trip.

3. How much time do I need to see a place?

Timing is crucial in Australia!

This is the most important element in crafting your ideal itinerary. You need to know the minimum time you're going to allot to each place.

Let's say you plan a visit to the Kakadu National Park. You need at least three to four days to do it justice (it's half the size of Switzerland!). So what if you only have one day? It's simple: Don't go to Kakadu National Park. Period. Instead, pick a sensible alternative that allows you to see a small national park just one hour's drive from Darwin.

4. How should I travel in Australia?

It's difficult to determine travel distances from the map. What looks like a short distance often turns out to be a several-day trip. Australia is a great country for road trips, but it's crucial that you know what you're getting into beforehand.

Choose your self-drive destinations based on your level of driving experience. Keep in mind that four-wheel drive can be challenging, especially if you have no experience. Anyone, however, can do an Outback road trip on sealed roads with no problems - even if you're travelling alone! If you want to reach remote destinations, flying is your best option. Once there, you can hire a car or join a tour for your explorations.

So what are the next steps?

Once you have the itinerary set, you're halfway there. The next important step is to make a travel plan that allows you to see Australia within your budget and time frame.

You need to know how to make cost-effective choices and not

waste money. (It's easy to make mistakes when planning a trip if you don't know how things work in Australia.)

Now let's take a look at the three essential elements for creating an itinerary that allows you to maximize your time, fit in the right destinations, and discover Australia independently.

Australia Trip Planning Basics

There are three elements that will determine the success of your trip: timing, transportation, and destinations. In this section, I'll review each of these in-depth.

1. Timing

Whether your trip is two weeks or three months, timing is key. On one hand, you don't want to miss out on important things, but on the other hand, you don't want to stay too long in one place as you want to make the most of your time.

So how do you know how much time you need to allocate to each destination?

First-hand experience. And that's where I can help!

In 10 years of travel, I've tested several options, made mistakes and learned how things work. These are my suggestions from a solo point of view.

You might need to tweak these suggestions based on how you want to travel, what activities you plan, and whether you plan to travel alone or with a companion.

With that being said, here's how much time you need in these core destinations:

Great Ocean Road (G.O.R.)

If you're self-driving, plan at least two full days (if no extra activities are planned). Ideally, three days allows you to do more of the walks and spend a whole day at the 12 Apostles, which is really worth it.

Kangaroo Island

Three full days and three nights is ideal, and this includes a round trip of the island with several stops on your way from east to west and south to north.

Extend it to four or five days if you plan on longer walks and specialty activities like seeing wildlife, going on food & wine tours, horseback riding, sandboarding, kayaking, etc. I wouldn't plan a one-day trip to Kangaroo Island, as this allows you to see only a tiny fraction of what the island has to offer.

Uluru and Red Centre

You need two days/two nights for Uluru and two days/two nights for Kings Canyon. This amount of time allows you to see Uluru at sunrise and sunset, plus do all the main walks, visit the cultural centre, see Kata Tjuta at sunrise, and do one to two walks there, too. The same goes for Kings Canyon: To do the Rim Walk and soak in the atmosphere, you need at least two full days.

Top End - Kakadu National Park

For visiting Darwin, you need two full days, plus a minimum of three days for exploring Kakadu N.P. If you want to see Litchfield N.P. and Katherine Gorge, add two extra days.

North Tropical Queensland - Cairns

You need at least five days/five nights to do justice to this awesome area. If you can plan six to seven days, all the better. This includes a Great Barrier Reef tour, and daily tours to Cape Tribulation, Atherton Tablelands, and Cairns' surroundings.

Sydney, Melbourne

For both Sydney and Melbourne, I'd recommend three to five days, depending on what you plan to do there. To explore the city's surroundings like Royal N.P., the Blue Mountains, and Phillip Island, plan at least one additional day each.

Wilson Promontory

To visit Wilson Promontory, you'll need two days -- but three days would be ideal if you're planning to do the longer walks in the Tidal N.P.

Tasmania

Five days/five nights for a basic round trip with no long hiking trails. Seven days/seven nights is better, and 10 days ideal if you plan longer walks in national parks and want to explore all areas of the island.

Perth and the Margaret River Region

One or two days are enough for Perth. If you want to visit its surroundings, such as Fremantle, Cottesloe Beach, or Rottnest Island, add one extra day each.

You'll need at least four to five days for visiting the whole region, including Busselton, Cape Naturaliste, Dunsborough, Margaret River, Augusta, and Cape Leeuwin.

2. Transportation

Once you've identified which destinations you're visiting and how long you're spending in each one, the next step is to decide how you're going to get to and around your destination.

Self-driving is a flexible way of travelling around Australia, since you can adjust your stay as you like it, whereas flights and train journeys can't be easily changed.

Here are some transportation tips:

- **Book all domestic flights before leaving**: And only when you have a fixed itinerary. Changing the dates of an already-booked flight means paying for a new ticket, unless you have flexi-fare tickets that allow date changes. Rail and bus passes are great because they allow you to change the dates of your travel. Greyhound offers a variety of bus passes.

- **Calculate enough time for road trips**: And for connecting with other transportation. You don't want to miss flights or ferries, as this will mean increasing your costs and dealing with the hassle that comes with missing a connection. Plan to get to your destination city at least 5-8 hours before early morning flights or ferries. Google Maps can be helpful for calculating timing and getting a feel for distances. For trains, make sure you reach your destination the evening before.

I know from experience that you need to plan carefully when you travel alone, as you can't swap driving duties and need time to rest after a long drive. In my opinion, there's no better way to travel around than using a car or campervan. This will increase your freedom infinitely!

Here are some questions you probably have about driving in Australia…

What's driving in Australia like?

Driving is easier than what you might think. Outside of the cities, traffic is almost non-existent. In remote areas of the Outback, however, you certainly need a level of expertise and will need to be familiar with four-wheel drive.

All main Outback road trips are on bitumen roads for two-wheel drive. I find it easier to drive from Alice Springs to Kings Canyon and to Uluru than to drive along the Great Ocean road, which is full of bends and requires more concentration.

How do you choose road trips as a solo traveller?

If you're travelling on your own for the first time, I would:

• Choose short road trips: Start with a travel distance of 200-300km, like a round trip on Kangaroo Island.

• **Drive in a loop**: Select road trips that start from one city, continue on a route with several interesting stops, and return back to your starting point. Like Melbourne to Wilson

Promontory, Cairns to Cape Tribulation, or Perth to Margaret River.

- **Use two-wheel drive for Outback road trips**: On all bitumen roads, you can use a two-wheel drive car -- like the Uluru trip from Alice Springs. No special driving skills are required. Here is a link to the best road trips of Australia from the main cities: https://www.rockytravel.net/blog/best-day-trips-from-australian-cities/

What if I'd like to drive, but don't fancy driving completely alone?

You can look for a travel companion who can join you on a road trip, or you can join a tour. Hostel bulletin boards are a great way of making friends with other travellers. YHA hostels are a great way to meet fellow solo travellers - be sure to check out the bulletin board. You can also search online forums like Gumtree to find travel companions. If you have a travel companion you can consider longer road trips, depending on the level of confidence and driving experience you have.

What about long road trips?

I'd consider a long trip to be anything over 1,500km. To give you an idea of distances, the road trip from Alice Springs -Kings Canyon - Uluru - Alice Springs is about 1,000-1,200km.

If you want to embark on longer trips, like crossing Australia from Darwin to Adelaide, Cairns to Sydney, or Adelaide to Perth, I'd highly recommend travelling with a companion. Driving 3,000km on your own can be daunting if you have no experience. Bear in mind that to cover 2-3,000 km or more, you need to plan at least 10-15 days.

What if I don't feel like driving myself?

If you don't want to drive, you still have several options:

- **Public transportation**: While Eastern Australia is well connected by bus and train services, Western Australia's public transportation is limited to Perth's surroundings and a few destinations to the north.

- **Greyhound buses**: These are good for the Eastern Coast from Queensland to Victoria, and more regional bus services are offered state wide. Some routes in Western Australia are available, too.

- **Train services**: Trains are good, but they require plenty of time; outside of metropolitan areas, they run just a few times per week. The GHAN from Adelaide to Darwin runs once per week during the low season and twice per week during high season. If you decide to travel by train and have one to two months, I'd recommend getting a rail pass. You can learn more on this site page: https://www.rockytravel.net/train-travel-in-australia/

- **Flying**: This is the fastest way to reach your destination, but you'll still have to hire a car locally -- as that is the best way to explore a place independently and at your own pace.

- **Group tours**: There are hundreds of small tour companies operating locally in Australia. If you don't want to drive yourself, this is the best option. I've mostly tried day tours, on Rocky Travel site you find with my reviews and on the Resources Section you'll find my recommendations for tours.

I also run my own tours starting from February 2019:
https://www.rockytravel.net/australia-group-tours/

How do I know what type of transportation is right for me?

A basic rule for each trip is to try and find a balance among your methods of transportation. Remember that adventure goes hand in hand in travel, and stepping out of your comfort zone will often be the highlight of any trip.

So why not try out something new and go on an easy road trip, instead of spending the whole time on group tours? Try to diversify your ways of travel: include a few flights, one or two road trips, one or two short tours, a train trip, and a cruise or boat tour.

If you're travelling on your own for the first time, start with one-third of the time on your own and the rest of it on tours, or half of it on tours and half on your own.

The more you learn how to explore places on your own, the more independent you'll become, and the more you'll enjoy yourself.

When can a tour offer a better experience than I can have by myself?

Though I am a fan of independent travel, there definitely are specialty tours that offer high value. These include all kinds of activities: wildlife viewing, river cruising, whale watching, fishing, outdoor adventures, cultural explorations, and food and wine tasting. Such specialty tours are usually offered on a daily basis, and they share in-depth knowledge and show the hidden secrets of a place you wouldn't be able to experience otherwise.

So even if you don't like tours, I encourage you to join specialty tours that match your interests; they deliver value and enrich the overall experience.

If you need more advice, arrange a quick Skype consult with me. Check out this page with more information about how this consult will work.

3. Destinations

Choosing your destinations is the hardest part of any trip itinerary. To make it a little bit easier, think back to the questions you asked yourself at the beginning. What is the focus of your trip? What are you trying to get out of it?

With that in mind, make a list of 10 or more destinations you'd like to visit. Then pull out a map and think about your timeframe and transportation options.

These questions might help:

1. **What distances** can you drive to on your own? Will you need four-wheel drive?

2. **What alternative ways of transportation** can you consider? Train, bus, guided tours?

3. **How much time do you need to visit a place** or an area?

Once you've done that, it should be easier to cross some destinations off your list and make a realistic itinerary. If you have three or four weeks for your trip, reduce the list to four or five destinations.

To help you further, I'll address a few common questions about destinations below.

Should I visit iconic attractions or places that are off-the-beaten path?

First off, you don't have to include "iconic attractions" on your itinerary just for the sake it.

If you don't like the city buzz, it makes sense to invest only a day or two visiting cities, with the rest of your time hiking in national parks, exploring the Outback, or chilling at the beach.

If you love wildlife, you should visit places like the G.O.R., Kangaroo Island or Outback, where you can see Australian animals. If you're a foodie, then places like Margaret River, North Tropical Queensland, and South Australia will be the perfect match.

Choose destinations that are meaningful to you and that match your interests, rather than trying to hit up every tourist attraction.

Are there any "must see destinations" in Australia?

Yes and no. Certainly there are destinations that are unique to Australia; and because they're so special, I think they're destinations that everyone should experience when visiting. Uluru, the Great Barrier Reef with the Daintree Rainforest, the Great Ocean Road, Fraser Island, the Kimberley and Shark Bay are top destinations.

But again, plan according to what appeals to you. If water isn't your friend and you don't particularly like marine life, just one day on the reef will give you a taste of the place. You can plan other activities in the Daintree rainforest, or select a food and heritage road trip in North Tropical Queensland.

Is Uluru (Ayers Rock) worth it?

To Uluru or not to Uluru. Some people are underwhelmed when they visit Uluru -- but how can one of the most iconic attractions of Australia be disappointing?

Weather conditions and the time of year play an important role in visiting Uluru. If you plan your trip to Australia in December through February, be prepared for temperatures of 40°C or greater. June through August is the high season, due to its pleasant temperatures. That being said, dozens of buses and hundreds of tourists don't make for the best environment to visit Uluru.

To savour the peacefulness and the spirit of this place, you need to consider all this. Personally, I'd only plan a visit to Uluru in autumn (March-May), but if you have no other choice and really want to see it, then go!

Conclusion

I know it's not easy to choose your destinations, since you're afraid you might miss out on something great or fun.

On my first trip to Australia, there were no good resources online. My only tools were a Lonely Planet and a German guidebook; they helped me research and study all my options over a period of six months.

Now you won't need six months, or even six weeks to create your itinerary. With this book in hand, you'll need one hour to read it, plus a week to make your choices and put together a detailed itinerary.

In this book, I've included four main itineraries for first time solo travellers. Each one is based on my personal experience and knowledge about what is important to discover on a first time trip to Australia.

I'd suggest reading through all of the itineraries, then putting it aside for a few days. Once you've had time to reflect, go back and make a list of all the destinations that you feel called to.

Now for the fun part: The Itineraries!

Introduction to Australia Itineraries

I've created four itineraries to suit the needs of first time solo travellers to Australia.

They're targeted at solo travellers, travelling either alone or with a companion, at women travelling alone who want to discover the country in all its splendor, seeing iconic landmarks as well as immersing themselves into the local culture.

By going through each itinerary, you'll get a clear picture of what you want to do. They are built to help you identify the main areas and activities you want to focus on.

Each itinerary comes complete with clear and detailed information so you'll know whether it fits with your time frame, travel style, and budget.

And of course, each one can be fully customized and altered to your own needs and desires.

Each itinerary is organized the same way so you can easily locate the information you need.

At the end of each itinerary there are useful resources that will help you in your trip planning. From links to local visitor centres and useful websites to my recommendation about where to stay, how to book rental cars and choose day-trips or tours to add to your itinerary.

So not let's take a look at each individual Itinerary!

Itinerary no. 1. Iconic Australia

This itinerary is for the first time visitor to Australia who wants to see most of the iconic destinations and has three weeks. It's a well-balanced trip with a focus on nature, wildlife, and outdoor activities. You'll visit Sydney, Melbourne, Adelaide, the Great

Photo Gallery Itinerary no. 1
Icons of Australia

Ocean Road (G.O.R), Kangaroo Island and the Red Centre. The itinerary includes three road trips by car or campervan. It does not require any special driving skills, as you drive on sealed roads. It allows you to visit further destinations, like the Great Barrier Reef, if you have an extra week.

I'd recommend planning your Australia trip in the low season (March-May or October-December), because it's not as busy as in summer, the weather is warm with temperatures around 25-

28°C, the wildflowers are blossoming, and it is the ideal time for bushwalking and other outdoor activities.

Trip Legs:

The first trip leg is focused on Melbourne, the GOR road trip, and the coastal road trip to Adelaide. It is about 1,000 km to do in four days and four nights, with an array of stops to enjoy the beauty of the GOR and discover interesting places like Mt. Gambier, the Coorong National Park, and Victor Harbour, before crossing over to Kangaroo Island.

The second trip leg includes three days on Kangaroo Island and Adelaide. Kangaroo Island involves a 300km road trip with unique wildlife experiences, walks in national parks, and the iconic Remarkable Rocks.

The third trip leg is based in the Red Centre with Uluru, Kings Canyon, and Kata Tjuta. This portion is a six-day journey into Australia's heart and Alice Springs.

Itinerary Pace:

This itinerary is for **the active solo traveller** who loves to be on the go and doesn't mind long hours of driving. You'll be driving for about 2,000km altogether, and if you add an extra trip leg to the Great Barrier Reef, you can add 600 km more.

You can add a tour instead of driving, but self-driving is more fun, and the freedom involved will be worth it.

Who is this trip for?

This itinerary is for the active solo traveller who loves nature, wildlife, and bushwalking. It is perfect for those who feel called to discovering the Australian Outback -- but at the same time want to explore Australian cities like Sydney and Melbourne.

Though this itinerary is fairly easy, **you must enjoy driving**. It does not require special driving skills, as all road trips are sealed roads. The Red Centre road trip is all on sealed road and is indeed an easy drive.

There are additional routes you can add to this itinerary, which you'll read all about in the customization section.

This itinerary encompasses the core destinations of Eastern Australia; this is where I started my travels here.

As for the cost estimate it can be anywhere from 3500 to 4500 Australian dollars on a budget and from 6000 to 8500 Australian dollars on a luxury trip. The cost of your trip will depend on the type of transportation and lodging you choose. By self-driving you will keep the cost down, whereas the more tours and activities you add the more expensive it will be.

As for the cost estimate, it can be anywhere from 3500 to 4500 Australian dollars on a budget, and from 6000 to 8500 Australian dollars on a luxury trip. The cost of your trip will depend on the type of transportation and lodging your choose. By self-driving, you'll keep the costs down, whereas the more tours and activities you add, the more expensive it will be.

To dig deeper and calculate the cost of your itinerary, check out the resource page and get in touch with me for advice.

This is an overview of the itinerary highlighting the road trips from Melbourne to Adelaide along the GOR and K.I and Adelaide (A-G), the Outback road trip (A-D), and the internal flights from Adelaide to Alice Springs and Ayers Rock to Sydney. You can view this Google Map by using this link: https://bit.ly/2uOLm7B

Itinerary Trip Legs

Melbourne

Your trip starts in Melbourne, where your international flight arrives. Here are my picks for visiting Melbourne.
Federation Square is Melbourne's hub. From the Visitor Centre to the Ian Pottery Centre, you'll find the heartbeat of the city here.
South Bank Complex is a must: It features a river promenade, shopping malls, city markets, and Eureka Tower.
Arcades & Lanes are what Melbourne is famous for. Its hidden lanes with rich history, traditions, and cultural flair. Explore them alone or on a guided tour.
State Library & Victoria Markets
are two unmissable icons. Check out these live on the web here: https://www.rockytravel.net/blog/20-things-to-do-in-melbourne/

Great Ocean Road

This is a three-day road trip with stunning coastal views, a unique landscape, and rich vegetation.

Geelong is about 70km from Melbourne. Stop here to grab maps of the area, as well as brochures and information about your Great Ocean Road trip.

Torquay is a little village with a nice promenade walk and Sunday Markets. A few minutes south of Torquay, stop to view

Bells Beach. In **Anglesea**, follow the sign for the golf club to see kangaroos grazing on the fields.

Lorne is your next stop, which is a great place for staying overnight, surfing, or just watching surfers. On your way to Apollo Bay, don't miss out on the **Kennet Koala Walk**. There's a sign on the road to turn right where the camping site is. This is a great place to spot koalas perched on eucalyptus trees.

Otway National Park offers various walks. You need to plan a half to a full day here if you love walking in the forest.

On your way to the National Park, take a detour to the **Cape Otway Lighthouse** (about 20km); this hidden area is a great place to spot koalas and native animals.

Next stop is 12 Apostles Visitor Centre in Port Campbell. From the visitor's centre, you can view the seven wave sculptured limestone stacks. Plan at least 5-8 hours to visit this magnificent area.

Click to view this itinerary live on the Google Map:
https://bit.ly/2GGDoip

Coastal Drive to South Australia

From Port Campbell to Cape Jervish is a good 600km drive. On your way, stop at Port Fairy to stay overnight.

Visit Mt. Gambier to see the blue lake and the volcanic complex, with caves and beautiful sinkholes (gardens).

Stop at Kingston for the best fish and chips in Australia. On your way, the Coorong National Park offers interesting and unique walks in the marine park and bush tucker aboriginal tours.

Stay in Victor Harbour overnight before leaving the mainland to board the **Sealink Ferry** from **Cape Jervish** to **Penneshaw**, where you'll start your three-day road trip around Kangaroo Island.

Kangaroo Island

On Kangaroo Island, stop at Penneshaw Tourist Information Centre to get maps and information about the island.

Next up is **Seal Bay** to see the sea lions and the natural park. I recommend the 30-minute guided tour to learn about the sea lion colony living on K.I. It's a unique experience! Stay overnight in **Vivonne Bay**, which is a great place for budget accommodation. Stop at Little Sahara to see the huge sand dunes. If you like sandboarding, you'll have fun here! Spend time at **Hanson Bay beach.**

With its coastal park, this is an iconic attraction on K.I. It's about one hour drive from Flinders Chase National Park. Plan at least one full day for visiting the Remarkable Rocks and Admiral Arch, there are over 24 walking trails in the park (everything from short walks to multi-day hikes).For **close wildlife encounters**, stop at **Parndana Wildlife Sanctuary** on the way to Kingscote on the north eastern side of the island.

Visit the **Ligurian Honey Farm**, taste wine at **Bay of Shoals Winery**, and take a stroll through the harbour.

You can read about about my three-day here live on the web: https://www.rockytravel.net/blog/re-discovering-kangaroo-island/

You can view this itinerary live on the web: https://bit.ly/2HeOA6Q

Next stop is Adelaide, where you'll catch your two-hour flight to the Red Centre. Plan two full days to see **Adelaide** and enjoy the city vibe with its parklands, city beaches, and iconic central markets. Check out this post on the top things to do in Adelaide: https://www.rockytravel.net/blog/things-to-do-in-adelaide/

Red Centre of Australia

Alice Springs is the capital of Central Australia, and it's worth spending a whole day here visiting the Old Telegraph Station and viewing the city from Anzac Hill. You'll also find the best aboriginal art galleries in Australia. Don't miss out on **Alice Spring Desert Park** and the **Flying Doctors Museum**. From Alice Springs, you start your second road trip, which is fully on sealed roads.

The first stop is **Kings Canyon**, where you spend two days and two nights. Start the **Kings Canyon Rim Walk** as early as you can in the morning (five hours).

After staying at Kings Canyon Resort, set off for Yulara resort to explore **Uluru** and **Kata Tjuta** (300 km away). It's good to get there in the late afternoon so you can witness the sunset that evening and the sunrise the next morning. Plan your drive to get there on time, as the viewing platform is 15 km away from the sunset platform.

Don't miss out on the free morning walk offered by the rangers, which is usually at 8 am. You can then continue on your own to the **Uluru Base Walk.** (Check with the visitor's centre).

For more tips on what to do at Uluru check out these tips: https://www.rockytravel.net/blog/tips-for-visiting-uluru/

Sydney

Spend three days visiting **Sydney City** and its magnificent Harbour. Visit the **Opera House**; guided tours run hourly. Walk along the Harbour Bridge, or go on a climbing tour if you feel adventurous.

Take the **ferry from Circular Quay to Manly** and return at dusk to enjoy a magnificent sunset over Sydney Harbour and the city.

Go for a beach **walk from Bronte to Bondi** (2km) or Coogee to Bondi (5km). If you love walking, take the Spit Bridge to Manly (10 km) from the northern side of the harbour for a breathtaking view over the city. Visit the Taronga Zoo, the Botanical Gardens and Hyde's Park. To get around, use the free city bus hop on/hop off no. 555 and public transport. You can also hire a bike or walk.

Stay, dine, and shop at **The Rocks** close to the Opera House.

You can also go **on a scenic flight** and see Sydney from the air. Check out this post for more Things to do in Sydney: https://www.rockytravel.net/blog/fun-things-to-do-in-sydney-activities/

Your 21-day Icons of Australia itinerary ends in Sydney, where your flight takes you back home.

If you have questions or need a quick consult on your itinerary, get in touch with me by sending in your email to Michela: info@rockytravel.net

A Recap of the Itinerary

The **Icons of Australia itinerary** takes you from South Eastern Australia to the Red Centre and back to Sydney. You'll see three major natural wonders and the three main cities of Australia. On this itinerary, you will:

- **Drive along the G.O.R**, 300km coastal scenery.

- **Explore Kangaroo Island** on your own.

- **Observe wildlife** on road trips.

- **Road trip to the Red Centre** Uluru + Kings Canyon.

- **Enjoy the city buzz** Melbourne, Sydney.

Check out this short review to see whether you remember everything this itinerary has to offer. Click on the arrow to scroll through the eight multiple-choice questions. The green button shows the correct answer. Have fun!

Does the itinerary match your expectations in terms of destinations and travel style, but you don't have three weeks time? Or perhaps you have more time, and are wondering how to fill your extra days! If so, read on for some itinerary customizations.

Customization Options

A 2-week Itinerary

I wouldn't recommend going to Australia for two weeks on your first trip. But if that's all you can swing, here are some options for you:

- **Fly from Adelaide to Ayers Rock** and skip the Kangaroo Island road trip. You'll save four days, but still maintain the original plan to see Uluru. By shortening your stay in the cities, you reduce your trip from 21 to 14 days! You can't reduce your stay at Uluru as you need at least two nights/two days to witness the sunrise/sunset at both locations (Uluru and Kata Tjuta), as well as enjoy a couple of walks around the Uluru and at Kata Tjuta.

Extended Itinerary

If you have more time to spend (lucky you!), you can extend your stay by adding specialty tours or more activities you love.

Here are a few ideas:

- **Extend your stay in Melbourne and Sydney**: These cities offer an abundance of activities. From Sydney, you can take day trips to the Blue Mountains, the Royal National Park, or the northern beaches. The same goes for Melbourne: by adding one day, you can enjoy a day tour to Phillip Island, visit the island and see the unique Penguin Parade.

- **Add extra days to your road trips**: If you plan to do more walks on the GOR, add one extra day to this road trip. If you'd like to go on food tours, add one extra day on Kangaroo Island. In Alice Springs, you can add an extra day for a trip to the Western Mc Donnell Ranges, where you'll see stunning landscapes and gorges.

- **Take the train from Adelaide to Alice Springs**: If you can add in one or two days, why not travel by train o the GHAN? This is a great way to make your journey a real experience. I've done it three times and loved it. It takes 24 hours, so you spend a full day on the train. Note that the train only leaves once a week from September to May (on Sundays) and twice a week from June to August. It also gets very busy during school holidays.

Add or change a trip leg

If you have another week to add to the original itinerary, you can extend your stay and plan a flight to **Tropical North Australia** and include **Cairns** and its surroundings. This may include a tour to the **Great Barrier Reef**, as well as short road trips to Cape Tribulation, Cooktown and the Atherton Tablelands. You need six full days for this extra trip leg.

Alternatively, you can add a visit to the Grampians National Park after completing the GOR road trip. This is an alternative way to get to Cape Jervish or Adelaide. Instead of driving along the coast, you'll take an inland detour; this is definitely worth doing if you're keen on hiking and camping.

Add a tour

Don't forget that you can swap any road trip with a tour. From personal experience, these three road trips are easy -- but if I had to rate them, I'd call Kangaroo Island the easiest and most relaxing route, followed by Alice-Springs to Ayers Rock.

The GOR road trip is the longest and most demanding in terms of length, drive time and driving experience. If it's not appealing to you, maybe select a three-or-four-day-adventure tour on Kangaroo Island* or a tour to Ayers Rock.*

This will cost you more, so I'd only recommend this option if you don't feel confident driving by yourself. (I've done them on my own -- and if I can do it, you can, too!)

Travel Resources to Itinerary no. 1.

Travel Websites Victoria

Visit the Fderation Square Info Point the largest and most-visitor-friendly Info Point of Australia. Check out for this site with a list of all Victoria Visitor Centres:
https://www.visitgreatoceanroad.org.au/visitor-information-centres

Getting around Victoria

Free CBD trams and a 5$day bus service check out this page:
http://www.melbourne.vic.gov.au/parking-and-transport/public-transport/Pages/public-transport.aspx

For your G.O.R road trip I'd recommend hiring a car:
https://www.rockytravel.net/DriveNow

Accommodation in Victoria

I recommend staying at the YHA Melbourne Central for a budget stay, here is the link : https://booki.ng/2IwtT5B

For private rooms/apartments use Airbnb you can get 30 USD off your first booking with my link: https://www.airbnb.com/c/mfantinel

Tours in Melbourne

I recommend the free-guided walking tours. You need to book yourself in though. Here is the link:
http://fedsquare.com/shopvisit/guided-tours

Travel Websites South Australia

Main Visitor Centre is the Rundle Mall. for local events ant the Adelaide Central Markets Website.

Getting around S.A

Use the free tram services, here is the link:
https://www.adelaidemetro.com.au/Timetables-Maps/Special-Services/Free-City-Services

You can also use the free bikes services to get around in Adelaide.

For travelling to Kangaroo Island use the Sealink for Ferry+Bus Transfer from Adelaide to Kangaroo Island.

Car Rentals on Kangaroo Island use this link:
https://www.rockytravel.net/DriveNow

Flights from Adelaide to Alice Springs check out this link: https://rockytravel.net/Wotif-Flights

Accommodation in South Australia

I recommend staying at the YHA CENTRAL In Adelaide, here is the link to check their site: https://booki.ng/2Iws48N

On Kangaroo Island I stayed at Vivonne Bay Lodge, is a great place for a budget stay (very clean room with shared bathroom and a fabulous kitchen).

Here is the link for booking your stay on the Kangaroo Island: https://booki.ng/2GHcCq1

Tours on Kangaroo Island: Day-Tours on K.I. Here is the link:

Getting Around South Australia

For self-drive I strongly recommend hiring a car on the island soon after your arrival in Penneshaw. A car is the best, however if you plan a longer stay, like a week or longer, than a campervan could be the best choice. Here is the link for booking your car on the island.

Car Rentals on Kangaroo Island: https://www.rockytravel.net/DriveNow

Uluru and Red Centre

I recommend staying at the Outback Pioneer Hotel (hotel) or the Outback Pioneer Lodge (budget) here is the link to the booking site : https://booki.ng/2IydSwh

For the Kings Canyon Resort I recommend these places that you can check out here : https://booki.ng/2sTUrWX

Travel Websites New South Wales

For The Sydney Visitor check out this page:
https://www.property.nsw.gov.au/visitors

Free apps to download:

Sydney Walks and Maps
https://apple.co/2IvSw2o

Multi-lingual Sydney City Maps:
https://apple.co/2JmnQC9

Sydney Map + Sydney Airport
https://apple.co/2GImOOM

Getting Around in Sydney

There is a **Free Bus service 555** in the city, it's free and the services runs every 10 minutes from Central Station to Circular Quay back in a loop. If you are planning to use public transportation in Sydney I highly recommend you get an OPAL CARD (free) as this allows you to buy day-passes and more discounts on ferries.

On Sunday there is a 2.5 dollar cap to use it all day long as much as you want. It's really a great deal, bear on mind that one way-ticket on the Sydney Harbour will cost you 5-15 dollars depending on the length of your trip!

Here is the link to the page where you can find all information about the Bus Services in Sydney: https://transportnsw.info/

Accommodation in N.S.W

For Budget Accommodation I recommend this boutique hostel: YHA Sydney Harbour: https://booki.ng/2l6hdsE

For hotels I recommend this hotel near Circular Quay: https://booki.ng/2sMsiTZ

For private rooms/apartments use Airbnb.com You can get a 35 USD voucher on your first booking, if you sign up with this link:

https://www.airbnb.com/c/mfantinel

Tours in Sydney

For Tours in Sydney check out this link: https://www.partner.viator.com/en/10250/Sydney/d357-ttd

Itinerary no. 2. The Eastern Coast

No trip to Australia is complete without a visit to the Northeast Coast. That being said, this coast stretches from Brisbane to Cairns (over 2,000 km), so you need to make some hard

Photo Gallery Itinerary no. 2
The Eastern Coast

choices about what you want to see there.

This itinerary gives you the opportunity to see not only the iconic Great Barrier Reef, but also to discover unique places like Fraser Island and the Daintree Rainforest in North Tropical Queensland. If you love the beach and water sports, Queensland offers a wealth of activities from surfing, diving, and snorkeling to kayaking, board paddling, hang gliding, ocean skydiving, and more.
The itinerary is made of three trip legs and includes five days in

Sydney, which is your arrival and departure port. It's a great combination of cities, beaches, and iconic natural landmarks.

Trip Legs:

The first trip leg is anchored around Sydney City and includes a day-tour to the Northern Beaches, the Blue Mountains, and the Royal Park, along with visiting Sydney icons and Sydney beaches. It's not only about the city buzz -- there are plenty of walks and outdoor activities, too.

The second trip leg is focused on the triangle of Brisbane, the Sunshine Coast, and Fraser Island. It includes two days visiting the Sunshine Coast and a three-day tour on Fraser Island.

The third trip leg is focused on North Tropical Queensland, where you'll spend five days. This leg includes tours to the Great Barrier Reef and two road trips to the Atherton Tablelands and the northern Coast, Cape Tribulation, and further north to Cooktown.

Itinerary Pace:

This itinerary **goes at an active pace**: You'll be travelling around cities and will engage in lots of activities in nature -- everything from hiking in national parks and walking along the beach to swimming and snorkeling in the Great Barrier Reef. Don't worry: there will be time to relax, too!

Who is this trip for?

This itinerary is easy, and **anyone can do it on a solo trip**. Even if it's your first trip to Australia, it should be no problem for you. It doesn't require special driving skills because all the road trips are two-wheel-drive and within short distances. The total driving distance is about 600-1000km, but is spread out over several days.

This itinerary is for **the active beach and nature lover** who wants to discover Australia's coastline with its pretty beaches and coastal national parks, ancient rainforests, unique islands, and fascinating World Heritage sites.

Sydney is your arrival and departure point, and you'll have five days to enjoy the city and its surroundings.

If you're not keen on self-driving, you can go on guided tours or use alternative ways of transport to reach the destinations.

There are additional routes you can add to this itinerary and in the customization section, you can read about all the options. For personal advice and deeper insight, I can help you put together your dream itinerary.

This easy itinerary is a great choice if you're just starting travelling solo. It's also one of the least expensive itineraries, because you can make use of the extensive network of public transportation along the Eastern coast -- ranging from bus services to train journeys. The required budget starts at 2500 Australian dollars for 18 days, which includes tours to Fraser Island and the G.B.R. I would recommend this itinerary to adventurous female solo travellers who love the coastal landscape and everything related to the beach, the outdoors, and wildlife.

Take a look at the map overview on the following page, as well as each detailed trip leg. While you can do this itinerary throughout the year, the best time is March-May and Sept-Nov to avoid the crowd and the rain.

This is an overview of the Australia's Eastern Coast itinerary, which goes from Sydney and its surroundings to the Sunshine Coast and Fraser Island to North Tropical Queensland with Cairns.

Itinerary Trip Legs

Sydney

Sydney is a city where you can literally spend weeks without getting bored. Check out our list of fun things to do in Sydney

https://www.rockytravel.net/blog/fun-things-to-do-in-sydney-activities/

Here are some of my favorite spots in Sydney:

Day tours in Sydney's Surroundings

The Royal National Park is a very beautiful coastal national park, the second oldest in the world. It is only 30km from Sydney; you can drive there but the best way is to travel by train to Cronulla and cross over by ferry to Bundeena. The Marley Track takes you through stunning heathland, rock formations, and beaches.

Walk along the coastal cliffs to the amazing **Marley White Cliffs**, a.k.a. You can view it on this Google Map:

https://bit.ly/2l7JbUP

the "**Wedding Cake Cliffs**" to spot humpback whales (May-November). Jibbons Rock Tours are run by indigenous rangers; they're very informative about the bush tucker food.

Blue Mountains are a two-hour train journey from Sydney. This national park is a UNESCO World Heritage site, and there are many long and short walks to enjoy. I'd recommend at least a few days here. A day tour option is to **walk the Three Sisters Track** to Echo Point to view the Three Sisters mountains and witness a mysterious blue haze over the forest.

The Northern Beaches of Sydney are another great tour, as you'll see an array of stunning beaches. Take the bus from the city to Palm Beach and stop along your way at Dee Why Lagoon, Avalon, and Whale Beach.

From Whale Beach, you can also walk to Palm Beach and take a boat tour to the inlets and the Lighthouse.

Fraser Island

Your second leg of the trip is on the southern Queensland Coast, starting with the **Sunshine Coast**.
With its nice beaches, breathtaking sunsets, and nearby national parks, this is the ideal place to relax for a couple of days. Stay in **Noosa Heads**, from where you start your Fraser Island tour.

Fraser Island is the world's largest sand island and, with its unique ecosystem, is a must-do experience. You'll discover the island on 4WD, walk on sand dunes, swim in crystal clear lakes, ride across stretches of deserted beach, observe unique native animals (like dingos), go on night wildlife tours, and enjoy a pristine environment like no other. You can visit Fraser Island only by 4WD tour. No self-driving has been allowed on the island since 2010. I recommend at least a three-day tour to do justice to this awesome place.

Brisbane your final stop before leaving for Cairns. You can either rent a car and drive to Brisbane or travel by bus. In Brisbane, you'll spend two days and one night. **Southbank** is the popular district for locals and tourists, with a lovely park, walking paths, entertainment and museums, and markets. Excellent arts exhibitions are held throughout the year here. Walk along its beautiful bridges to reach the CBD. For information on what to do in Brisbane, you can check out this post: https://www.rockytravel.net/blog/visiting-brisbane-queensland/

Cairns, Great Barrier Reef and North Tropical Queensland

From Brisbane, fly out to Cairns to enjoy the last trip leg. Five days is the minimum time you should spend in this area -- and if you're able to extend your stay to 7-8 days, I'd highly recommend it.

That's because this area offers many short road trips and plenty of activities from daily to multi-day Great Barrier Reef tours. So if you want to go on a three-day GBR tour, you need to plan at least a week in this area. This itinerary includes the minimum time needed to suit female solo travellers with a three-week time frame. **Cairns** is the capital of North Tropical Queensland and the hub of your trip. Stay in Cairns, as this is where you'll start both of your road trips.

Road Trip to Cape Tribulation

This is an easy 200km daily tour going through **Port Douglas,** and it includes a forest walk at Mossman Gorge. Further north, you can go on a Daintree River boat tour to spot crocodiles and other wildlife, as well as cross over to **Cape Tribulation**.

The area is cut off from civilization and is a pristine environment for walking in the forest and relaxing on the beach. If you want to hide away for a while, plan a couple of extra days and stay overnight in Cape Tribulation. Just north of Moosman Gorge, you can turn left onto the road to Cooktown (200km).

You can view it on this Google Map: http://bit.ly/2LQAyJE

Continue your road trip with a visit to this ancient forest village and go on an indigenous rock art tour.

Road Trip to Atherton

A road trip to Atherton makes for a great day tour. Starting from Cairns, your first stops are the historical museum and famous boulders of Babinda. Keep driving to reach the Millaa Millaa Falls and further north to the Tablelands's lakes.

In this area, you can taste and buy the finest Australian organic tea. Stop at **Yungabarra** for the heritage walk and the 500-year-old Cathedral Fig Tree. Visit the volcanic lakes of Barrine and Ecacham, along with the **Crystal Caves.** You'll reach **Mareeba** 30km from Atherton, which is a tropical plantation paradise of mangos, lychees, bush cherries, and passion fruit. Visit **Skybury**, which is Australia oldest coffee plantation. From there you drive back to Cairns through **Kuranda** where you can visit Barron Falls. Here is a guide to North Tropical Queensland:

Itinerary Recap

This itinerary takes you from Sydney to the Sunshine Coast and beyond, to North Tropical Queensland and three UNESCO World Heritage sites. On this itinerary, you will:

• **Discover Sydney** and its surroundings

• **Explore Fraser Island** the largest sand island in the world.

• **Road trip through North Tropical Queensland** from Cairns to Cape Tribulation to the Atherton Tableland.

• **Explore the Daintree rainforest,** the most ancient rainforest of the world.

• **Snorkel on the G.B.R in Cairns,** the largest coral reef of the world

Does the itinerary match your expectations in terms of destinations and travel style, but you don't have three weeks time? Or perhaps you have more time, and are wondering how to fill your extra days. If so, read on for some itinerary customizations.

Customization Options

14-day Itinerary

With only two weeks, you'll need to make a choice in terms of destinations. I wouldn't go to all three destinations, as time is simply too tight. It's doable only if you decide to see Fraser Island on a two-day tour and reduce your stay in Sydney to four days, though you'll keep five days in Cairns.

- **To save time**, you could also **fly from Sydney to Cairns**. This way, you'll save time planned for Fraser Island and the Sunshine Coast and still reduce your visit to 14 days. You'll spend one week in the Sydney area and one week in Cairns.

If you plan a three-day tour to the Great Barrier Reef, the rest of the week can be used for road trips. Sydney offers plenty of things to do; and you can easily spend four days in the city and three days in the national parks or northern beaches surrounding it.

Extended Itinerary Options

My suggestion is to stick to the original itinerary and extend your stay two days in Sydney, two days in Cairns, and two or three days in the Brisbane area by adding a road trip to the Gold Coast or Byron Bay's beaches.

- **Extend your stay in the Brisbane area:** You could add a day tour to the Australia Zoo; if you love wildlife, this is an amazing zoo one hour by train from Brisbane. You could hire a car and go to Byron Bay to see its legendary beaches. If you want to see the buzz of the Gold Coast, Coolangatta is worth a visit.

- **Add extra days to your day trips:** I'd suggest adding one day to the Blue Mountains so you can do more of the walks. The Royal National Park also offers a wonderful 24km walking tour, which can be done over two days by staying overnight in the park. Here a blog post about 5 days trips from Sydney by public transportation:
  https://www.rockytravel.net/blog/day-trips-from-sydney/

- In the Cairns area, there are many destinations like **Green Island or Fitzroy Island** to relax. If you look for a good combination of walking, outdoor activities and beach relaxation, then Magnetic Island is a good pick. It all depends on what you want to do.

- If you want to **learn more about the indigenous culture** in Tropical North Australia, spend a few days in Cooktown. Alternatively Cape Tribulation, is a great spot for beach and forest walks.

Add or change a trip leg

This itinerary is built with three trip legs so you can travel slowly and maximize your experience. If you want to add or replace one trip leg, I'd suggest an Outback experience in Queensland. I wouldn't add any extra flights to this itinerary, since you already have three.

While the Outback experience will add a touch of diversity to your trip, consider an island tour if you love the beach and are looking for an opportunity to relax.

- Alternatively, you could replace the Sunshine Coast trip leg with one to the **Whitsunday Islands**. This is a great option if you're keen on diving, snorkeling, and sailing. There are great tours going out to the W.I. for three or four days. If you see the GBR here, you can then focus your trip in Cairns on other activities, like road trips.

  I'd recommend the Whitsunday Islands if you're travelling with a companion, but I wouldn't spend a long time there if you're travelling on your own. Cairns is definitely a better destination for solo travellers than the Whitsundays.

Transportation Options

The original itinerary is a great route for solo travellers, as you can do all of the road trips on your own and will be actively discovering places and meeting people on your way. It involves self-driving on two or three easy road trips, as well as three internal flights and local tours. If you travel with a companion, it's a piece of cake in terms of driving.

- You can consider catching a **train from Sydney to Brisbane**, and travel by bus from there to the Sunshine Coast. The train journey takes the entire day, but if you have time and don't want to fly too much within Australia, this is a good option. From Brisbane, you can go to the Sunshine Coast by bus or pick a Fraser Island tour that includes a pick-up from Brisbane (there are a few).

While Sydney is well connected by public transport to its surroundings (you don't need to hire a car to visit), in Cairns, you need a car or campervan. You can obviously choose to go on tours instead of self-driving, but I wouldn't recommend it. From Cairns, there is **bus service to Kuranda**, Cape

Tribulation, and more destinations, but you'll need 8-10 days minimum to visit the area by public transport.

Add a tour

For this itinerary, the only tours you need to choose are for the Great Barrier Reef, Fraser Island, and aboriginal culture. For all the remaining destinations, I wouldn't bother going on tours -- as you can explore everything by yourself.

No tour can replace the fun, freedom, and experience of a road trip. There are, however, a wealth of day tours and specialty tours that can enhance your road trip experience. I would definitely advise you to go with these types of tours, rather than a tour that covers the whole trip leg and thereby reduces your autonomy and freedom.

Travel Resources for Itinerary no. 2

Travel Websites New South Wales

For The Sydney Visitor check out this page:
https://www.property.nsw.gov.au/visitors

Free apps to download:

Sydney Walks and Maps
https://apple.co/2IvSw20

Multi-lingual Sydney City Maps:
https://apple.co/2JmnQC9

Sydney Map + Sydney Airport
https://apple.co/2GImOOM

Getting Around in Sydney

There is a **Free Bus service 555** in the city, it's free and the services runs every 10 minutes from Central Station to Circular Quay back in a loop. If you are planning to use public transportation in Sydney I highly recommend you get an OPAL CARD (free) as this allows you to buy day-passes and more discounts on ferries.

On Sunday there is a 2.5 dollar cap to use it all day long as much as you want. It's really a great deal, bear on mind that one way-ticket on the Sydney Harbour will cost you 5-15 dollars depending on the length of your trip!

Here is the link to the page where you can find all information about the Bus Services in Sydney: https://transportnsw.info/

Flying

Flights from Sydney
https://rockytravel.net/Wotif-Flights

Car Hire

Car Rentals from Sydney
https://www.rockytravel.net/DriveNow

Accommodation in N.S.W

For Budget Accommodation I recommend this boutique hostel: YHA Sydney Harbour: https://booki.ng/2l6hdsE

For hotels I recommend this hotel near Circular Quay:
https://booki.ng/2sMsiTZ

For private rooms/apartments use Airbnb.com You can get a 35 USD voucher on your first booking, if you sign up with this link:

https://www.airbnb.com/c/mfantinel

Tours in Sydney

For Tours in Sydney check out this link:
https://www.partner.viator.com/en/10250/Sydney/d357-ttd

Travel Websites Queensland

Cairns Visitor Centre
https://www.cairnsvisitorcentre.com/

Download a free Fraser Island Guide

https://www.npsr.qld.gov.au/parks/fraser/pdf/fraser-island-visitorguide.pdf

For Cairns and North Queensland check out this free app:

Getting around Queensland

Flying

For Flights from Cairns, fro Brisbane and from the Gold Coast
https://rockytravel.net/Wotif-Flights

Car Hire
Car Rentals from Cairns, Brisbane and Gold Coast
https://www.rockytravel.net/DriveNow

Accommodation in Queensland

For budget accommodation I use YHA Central in Cairns:
https://booki.ng/2JR5Q5P

For Hotels check out this page:
https://booki.ng/2JL9tqD

For private rooms/apartments use Airbnb.com You can get a 35 USD voucher on your first booking, if you sign up with my link:

https://www.airbnb.com/c/mfantinel

Tours of Queensland

Discounted 1-3 day Tours of Fraser Island

https://www.partner.viator.com/en/10250/search/fraser%20island

Discounted day tours of the Great Barrier Reef

https://www.partner.viator.com/en/10250/travel-tips/Great-Barrier-Reef-Tours/ttd

Day tours of Brisbane and surroundings

https://www.partner.viator.com/en/10250/Brisbane/d363-ttd

Inspiration from the Blog

https://www.rockytravel.net/blog/tag/tropical-north-queensland/

Itinerary no. 3 - From West to East

This itinerary is for food and nature lovers. It's one of my favourite routes. It stretches from the Western to the Eastern coast, starting from South Western Australia across to Victoria, covering over 4,000km of amazing landscapes and mild climates. This itinerary includes three easy road trips on sealed

Photo Gallery Itinerary no. 3
From West to East

roads and one guided Outback safari tour in South Australia. It's ideal for the female solo traveller who is willing to drive on her own but prefers short routes, is active in the outdoors, and wants to try local food and wine. While you can visit throughout the year (thanks to the mild climate), March through May and October through December are the ideal times. I'd recommend October through December, when the wildflower season starts.

It's a great time for walking, bird watching, and spotting humpback whales in South Western Australia with no crowds. I wouldn't travel in June through August, as weather may be unpleasant and cold in some regions.

Trip Legs:

The first trip Leg focuses on **South Western Australia** and starts in Perth. After a short visit to Western Australia's capital city, you'll head south to the **Margaret River region**. From Perth, it's 270km to reach Busselton. From Cape Naturaliste to Cape Leeuwin, the scenic Caves Road meanders through soft hills, rugged coastline, and over 150 wineries. In this thriving region, you'll taste the finest food and wines Australia has to offer, as well as enjoy local produce, walks into the forest and coastal heathland, sandy beaches, natural caves, and the marvelous Karri forest.

The second trip leg takes you through **South Australia**, including a three-day Outback safari to the **Flinders Ranges**, which is one of the most spectacular ancient Outback areas in Australia. You'll also enjoy a three-day road trip (self-driving) to **Kangaroo Island**, home to Australia's third largest sea lion colony and a wealth of endangered Australian animals.

The third trip leg is in **Victoria**, where you'll explore **Phillip Island** and **Wilson Promontory**. This part of the trip focuses on nature and wildlife. First up are the Penguin Parade, fur seals, and koalas of Phillip Island. Next are great walking trails in Tidal River National Park.

Trip Pace:

This itinerary requires a **good level of fitness**, as you'll be on the go for 25 days and spend two-thirds of your time on the road. There are three self-driving road trips and one guided Outback safari.

Who is this trip for?

This itinerary is for food and wine lovers, as well as nature lovers who want to do lots of walks, see lots of diverse landscape, and observe wildlife.

It's a great itinerary that can easily be extended or shortened. It doesn't require special driving skills, as all road trips are on sealed roads and are short. The longest drive (700-800km) is in Margaret River, and you can easily do it alone. Not to mention, the three-day Outback tour will give you a good break from these short road trips. I recommend picking one or two local tours if you want to better understand (and taste!) the region's food and wine, as well as hands-on courses in the Margaret River region or on Kangaroo Island, like cooking courses, "behind-the-scene" winery tour and more.

There are additional routes you can add to this itinerary, and in the customization section, you can read about all your options. I've done this itinerary and would do it again. It's a great trip that shows you the highlights of Southern Australia, while also giving you a taste of the Australian Outback. It's best if you can travel in the spring or fall, when you can see humpback whales off the coast and enjoy the wildflowers in bloom.

On a budget you will spend anything between 3500-4500 Australian dollars. If you go with more expensive accommodation like cottages, hotels and private apartments, or if you want to add more tours, the cost can go up to 7500 Australian dollars.

This itinerary is for food and nature lovers. It's one of my favourite routes. It stretches from the Western to the Eastern coast, starting from South Western Australia across to Victoria, covering over 4,000km of amazing landscapes and mild climates.

This itinerary includes three easy road trips on sealed roads and one guided Outback safari tour in South Australia. It's ideal for the female solo traveller who is willing to drive on her own but prefers short routes, is active in the outdoors, and wants to try local food and wine.

While you can visit throughout the year (thanks to the mild climate), March through May and October through December are the ideal times.

I'd recommend October through December, when the wildflower season starts. It's a great time for walking, bird watching, and spotting humpback whales in South Western Australia with no crowds. I wouldn't travel in June through August, as weather may be unpleasant and cold in some regions.

Itinerary Trip Legs

Perth

Upon your arrival in Perth, I'd recommend two days for visiting this city:

Kings Park, the largest city park in the world, is the jewel and soul of the city. Plan a full day. Check out my guide on things to do in Perth: https://www.rockytravel.net/blog/top-five-things-to-do-in-perth/

Fremantle, with its picturesque fishing port and crafts markets is a nice place for dining and walking at sunset.

Cottesloe Beach is Perth's most famous beach and is a popular spot for travellers and locals on weekends. Ideal for a beach walk or a swim.

Rottnest Island is worth a visit if you plan a longer stay. Take the ferry over and enjoy a car-free paradise with over 20 secluded beaches and bays. Here you can also see the Quokkas (little marsupials).

A Guide about Rottnest island: https://www.rockytravel.net/blog/things-to-do-on-rottnest-island/

Check out this itinerary on the Google Maps:
http://bit.ly/2LQAZ6C

Margaret River Region

Hire your car in Perth and head south. The Margaret River Region lies 300km southwest of Perth and stretches over 100km from Cape Naturaliste to Cape Leeuwin.

Stop in **Busselton** to view Western Australia's iconic **Busselton Jetty** and its unique underwater world full of coral. Spend one or two nights in **Dunsborough** to visit **Cape Naturaliste** National Park with its beautiful coastal walks and sheltered beaches at Eagle Bay.

With over 160 wineries, the finest food in the area, and an array of local farms and events, plan at least three full days in **Margaret River**. Start from the visitor's centre, where you can pick up a detailed map of the area. Be sure to go on a wine tasting tour.

Cape Leeuwin is the most south westerly mainland point in Australia, where two oceans (the Southern ocean and the Indian) meet. Visit the lighthouse and walk around the Water Wheel area.

Hamelin Bay is a beautiful and relaxing beach where you can spot giant mantra rays and enjoy a swim in calm waters. Drive along **Caves Road** to marvel at the majestic **Boranup Forest** and its amazing and tall Karri trees. Visit **Jewel Cave** to see a fascinating wonderland of underground limestone formations.

Here is my guide on how to discover the South Western Australia by car:

https://www.rockytravel.net/blog/discover-south-west-australia/

Outback Flinders Ranges

If you haven't experienced the Australian Outback, the Flinders Ranges are one of the best spots in Australia. On this three-day tour, you'll get to see an ancient land full of stunning landscapes and rock formations.

View this itinerary on Google Map: http://bit.ly/2JBRfvK

Wilpena Pound: View this majestic amphitheater and St. Mary's Peak (1300 mt) from the lookout in **Flinders National**

Park featuring four walks and 14 hiking trails.

Warren Gorge: Spot the yellow footed Rock Wallaby here.

Brachina Gorge: Colorful walls, stoney creeks beds, ancient red gums with hollow barks.

Bunyeroo Valley: Best viewed from Razorback lookout.

Parachilna Gorge: Don't miss the unique atmosphere of the Praire Hotel.

Morolana Scenic Drive: Go here and to the lookout for a spectacular sunset. Read about my Outback Tour here.

Kangaroo Island

This destination has been covered on Itinerary no.1.

Adelaide

I'd recommend two days and one night here.

Phillip Island

From Melbourne, this is an easy drive (about 140km). Two days on the island is advisable. Here's what to look out for:

Penguin Parade: This is why people visit Phillip Island, and it's truly worthwhile. See the world's smallest penguins going back to their burrows after a day out at sea. If you're lucky, you'll see 1,000 or more little penguins waddling across the beach at sunset. Certainly a unique experience to treasure forever.

Nobbys Centre: Just a five-minute drive from the Penguin Parade, you can see fur seals from large screens inside the centre. Walk around on the raised boardwalk to spot dolphins and see little penguins in their burrows.

Koala Conservation Centre:
See koalas, kookaburras, and other animals in their natural habitat.

View this itinerary on Google Maps: http://bit.ly/2JNlnQV

Wilson Promontory

From Phillip Island, your road trip proceeds along the coast to Wilson Promontory. I'd suggest staying in **Yanakie** in the **Corner Inlet Marine National Park**, which is a short 25-minute drive from Tidal River National Park. The park offers over 20 walking trails from one to four hours to multi-day hikes. The easy short walks start from the Tidal River Visitor Centre and take you through the highest point of Tidal Overlook, from where you can see **Squeaky Beach** and Norman Bay. Don't miss the walk down to Squeaky Beach; it is one of the most beautiful beaches I have ever been to.

The wildlife walk (4km) is on your way back to Yanakie and is a great way to see kangaroos and many more animals in the wild. Two full days is the minimum you can spend in Wilson Promontory.

Here is my Solo Road Trip Adventure at Wilsons Promontory:

www.rockytravel.net/blog/solo-road-trip-to-wilson-promontory/

Itinerary Recap

The itinerary no. 3 From West to East itinerary allows you to cross the country, all while exploring the great regions of South Western Australia and South Australia. On this itinerary, you will:

- **Tour South Western Australia** with food and wine tastings and outdoor activities like walking, hiking, kayaking, swimming, and more.

- **Discover Kangaroo Island** on a self-driving tour.

- **Experience the real Outback** on a three-day tour in the Flinders Ranges.

- **Encounter wildlife** like kangaroos, rock wallabies, quokkas, giant manta rays, and penguins.

- **Hike in Tidal River N.P.** on the Wilson Promontory

Customization Options

17-day Itinerary

To shorten this itinerary, you'll have to eliminate one of the three trip legs. Don't reduce your time in Margaret River; three to five days is the minimum time for visiting.

Here are my recommended time-savers:

- **Fly from Perth to Adelaide**: You'll save the two days of train travel planned on the Indian Pacific.

- **Eliminate one of the trip legs**: I would plan two days in Perth, five days in Margaret River, and one week in South Australia with Kangaroo Island and the Flinders Ranges. Another option would be to spend one week in S.W.A. and one week in Victoria visiting Phillip Island and Wilson Promontory.

Extended Itinerary

I'd add more days to Margaret River and Wilson Promontory, as there are plenty of outdoor activities on offer.

Here are some ideas:

- **Plan more time for walking**: Explore a section of the Cape to Cape Track in the Margaret River Region. Or plan two or three more walks in Wilson Promontory.

- **Food events**: If food or cultural events are happening, plan extra days and make the most of it. Check Margaret River and Adelaide events calendars and extend your stay accordingly.

- **Spend more time in cities**: Adelaide and Melbourne are great cities for food tours, shopping, events, and cultural entertainment. It's worth checking the events calendar before you go.

Add or change a trip leg

If you **have at least one extra week**, I'd add a few days to South Western Australia with an extension of your road trip to Albany, Denmark, Walpole.

Here you can read more about it:
https://www.rockytravel.net/blog/albany-western-australia/

The scenery is spectacular: you'll see some of the prettiest rugged beaches and drive through the lush Karri Trees Forest. You can return to Perth on the inland route, too.

You can add a trip leg from **Adelaide to Melbourne** and drive along the **Great Ocean Road**. This is another great way to avoid flying and do one of the most spectacular coastal drives in Australia. It's a 1000km drive though, so you must be prepared to add an additional 1000km of self-driving to the existing route.

Add a Barossa Valley Food & Wine Tour, if you're interested in food and wine tastings.

If you prefer the city, do a day tour to visit more of **Adelaide's surroundings** like Port Adelaide, Victor Harbour, and Adelaide Hills.

Likewise, you can choose to go on a Yorke Peninsula Tours to see dolphins and migrating whales. If travelling alone, I'd recommend going on a tour to take a break from driving.

Transportation Options

For the three regions in this itinerary, self-driving is really the only way to go. As a solo traveller, you can certainly go on a tour, but I wouldn't do it for the entire duration of the trip. Maintain a healthy mix by choosing tours only for the more challenging areas, such as the Flinders Ranges.

Bottom line: you'll need a car to visit. You may prefer hiring a camper van and staying in campsites rather than hotels.

You can go on day tours to gain more in-depth knowledge of

the area. Choose tours that give you an overview of the area or offer hands-on experiences and tastings you can't do on your own, then continue to discover the place at your own pace. Check out the resources page for more tips on tours.

Here there are more options for finding the transportation that most suits you:

- **Flying instead of travelling by train**: If you don't fancy spending two days and two nights on the Indian Pacific, you can cover the 2,300km distance in a 2.5-hour flight from Perth.

- Instead of taking the train from Adelaide to Melbourne, you can either **drive yourself along the GOR** or fly. By airplane, you'll reach Melbourne in less than one hour. This is good if your time frame is tight and you don't want to spend much time getting to your destination.

The train journey is definitely more of an **Aussie experience**, however, so I would have a go if you want to try out something different.

As for accommodation, if camping is not your thing, private accommodation or serviced apartments (cottages) are the best choice in all three regions.

Travel Resources to Itinerary no. 3

Travel Websites S.W.A

Margaret River Visitor Centre
Grab the gorgeous Margaret River Map with detailed info about

wineries, events, things to do, local producers, markets:
https://www.margaretriver.com/events/

Getting Around S. W.A.

Perth City

Use the free bus service (yellow, blue and red cat buses) to get around Perth. Here is the link:
http://www.transperth.wa.gov.au/Timetables/PerthCATLiveTimes

Buses to Perth's surroundings: http://transwa.wa.gov.au/

Train Services:http://www.railmaps.com.au/journey_results.php?Origin=Perth

Flying

For Flights from Perth
https://rockytravel.net/Wotif-Flights

Car Hire

Car Rentals from Perth
https://www.rockytravel.net/DriveNow

Accommodation in S.West Australia

I recommend the Goodearth Hotel:
https://booki.ng/2HOXaYE

Margaret River I stayed at the Darby Serviced Apartment:
https://booki.ng/2MtoJXZ

For private rooms/apartments in Perth and West Australia use Airbnb.com. You can get a 35 USD voucher on your first

booking, if you sign up with this link:
https://www.airbnb.com/c/mfantinel

Tours of Margaret River

For a Food & wine tour Margaret River. I recommend this tour:
https://www.partner.viator.com/en/10250/tours/Busselton/Margaret-River-Small-Group-Food-and-Wine-Tasting-Tour/d23522-11231P1

Or you can browse through this tour list here:
https://www.partner.viator.com/en/10250/Margaret-River-tours/Food-Tours/d24851-g6-c80

Inspiration from the Rocky Travel Blog
You can read about my experience:
www.rockytravel.net/blog/exploring-the-margaret-river-region/

Travel Websites South Australia

Adelaide

The main Visitor Centre is the Rundle Mall.

Must visit place: The Adelaide Central Market
www.adelaidecentralmarket.com.au

How to travel around

Use the free trams:
https://www.adelaidemetro.com.au/Timetables-Maps/Special-Services/Free-City-Services

And the free bike hire service:
https://www.bikesa.asn.au/adelaidefreebikes

Kangaroo Island

From Adelaide to Kangaroo island book the bus-transfer to Cape Jervish + ferry to Penneshaw (Kangaroo Island) with: https://www.sealink.com.au/

Flying

Flights from Adelaide
https://rockytravel.net/Wotif-Flights

Car Hire

Car Rentals from Adelaide
https://www.rockytravel.net/DriveNow

Accommodation in South Australia

I recommend the YHA Hostel in Adelaide :
https://booki.ng/2sXyNmK

On K.Island I recommend the Seafront Hotel in Penneshaw:
https://booki.ng/2JFTFcU

Or use this page for more accommodation options on K.I.:
https://booki.ng/2JMs9pT

Tours on Kangaroo Island: Day-Tours on Kangaroo Island.

Tours of South Australia

I recommend the Sea Lion Tour, Seal Bay, Kangaroo Island:

http://www.sealbay.sa.gov.au/plan-your-visit/tour-prices-times

If you prefer going to Kangaroo Island with a group, this is a great 2-day tour from Adelaide:

https://www.partner.viator.com/en/10250/tours/Adelaide/2-Day-Kangaroo-Island-Tour-from-Adelaide/d376-5704CCCC

Flinders Ranges Tours

To discover the Flinders Ranges I recommend this 4WD adventure:

https://www.partner.viator.com/en/10250/tours/Adelaide/3-Day-Small-Group-Eco-Tour-from-Adelaide-Flinders-Ranges/d376-5734HB4

Inspiration from the Blog

www.rockytravel.net/blog/things-to-do-in-adelaide/
https://www.rockytravel.net/blog/re-discovering-kangaroo-island/

Travel Websites Victoria

Visit the Fderation Square Info Point the largest and most-visitor-friendly Info Point of Australia. Check out for this site with a list of all Victoria Visitor Centres:
https://www.visitgreatoceanroad.org.au/visitor-information-centres

Download the Free City 2 Go App for each city and region in Australia (works online and offline) https://apple.co/2Mk8Rdj

Getting around Victoria

Free CBD trams and a 5 $ day bus service check out this page:
http://www.melbourne.vic.gov.au/parking-and-transport/public-transport/Pages/public-transport.aspx

Phillip island

The interactive map:
http://www.visitphillipislandmap.com.au/

The Penguin Nature Parks including the Parade, Nobbies
Centre, Koala Conservation Centre and more nature parks.
Here is the link: https://www.penguins.org.au/

Accommodation in Victoria

I recommend staying at the YHA Melbourne Central for a
budget stay, here is the link : https://booki.ng/2IwtT5B

For private rooms/apartments use Airbnb you can get 30 USD
off your first booking with my link: https://www.airbnb.com/c/mfantinel

Tours in Melbourne

I recommend the free-guided walking tours. You need to book
yourself in though. Here is the link:
http://fedsquare.com/shopvisit/guided-tours

Tours of Victoria

Phillip Island

Book a pass for the Penguin Parade and access all nature parks:

https://bit.ly/2ld1yro

Wilsons Promontory National Park

List of walks

http://parkweb.vic.gov.au/explore/parks/wilsons-promontory-national-park/things-to-do/day-walks

Accommodation Guide at Tidal River

http://parkweb.vic.gov.au/__data/assets/pdf_file/0006/316968/WPNP-Accommodation-and-Camping-Guide.pdf

Inspiration from the Blog

You can read about my experience:

www.rockytravel.net/blog/solo-road-trip-to-wilson-promontory/

https://www.rockytravel.net/blog/wilsons-promontory-walks/

https://www.rockytravel.net/blog/1000-steps-walk-dandenongs/

Itinerary no. 4 - The Outback

This itinerary covers the best places in the Australian Outback, with everything from iconic destinations to hidden gems. It takes you through the most diverse Outback landscape, from grassland vastness to red, dusty plains to rugged ocean rock formations. You'll spend 90% of your time in the great outdoors

Photo Gallery Itinerary no. 4
Australia's Ancient Outback

of the Australian Outback.

You'll get around by car, train and plane. Though there are options for longer road trips with four-wheel-drive, the self-driving road trips are on sealed roads.

This is a great itinerary if you want to discover ancient Outback areas of Western Australia and the Northern Territory, an ancient landscape with a rugged beauty rich in colour and contrasts.

It's perfect for you if you've already seen some of the classic iconic destinations and don't feel like spending time in the cities or suburban areas.

This itinerary is best during winter (May-September), when the weather is warm with sunny days and cooler nights. In summer (November-March), some places won't be accessible due to rains and closed roads.

Trip Legs

The first trip leg focuses on the Top End of Australia; you'll travel onboard **the GHAN train** from Adelaide to Darwin. You'll stop in Alice Springs for one week, then go on a self-driving road trip to the **Red Centre of Australia**. You'll continue with your rail journey to Darwin and go to the **Kakadu National Park** on a 4WD tour.

The second trip leg takes you from the Northern Territory to **Kununurra** and the **Eastern Kimberley**. After three days, you'll fly to Broome in North Western Australia.

The third trip leg includes the **Fringe Coral Coast** of Western Australia, as well as Shark Bay, Shell Beach, and Monkey Mia. You'll visit this area by car on a five-day road trip. Your trip ends with a flight to Perth, from which you'll return home.

Trip Pace

This trip is definitely for the very active traveller. You'll be driving on your own across Outback areas and 90% of your time will be spent outdoors: in national parks, ancient and partly isolated outback areas in Northern Australia, and isolated coastal areas of Western Australia.

Who is this trip for

This itinerary focuses on the Australian Outback. It's for the active and adventurous female traveller who has already experienced self-driving trips on her own, feel called to discovering the Australian Outback, has some experience with self-driving, and doesn't mind being in isolated areas.

It's easy to get around and you must enjoy driving. It does not require special driving skills as all road trips are sealed roads. Also the Red Centre Road Trip is all on sealed roads as well as the coastal areas of Western Australia.

Alternatively, you can go on tours. You can check out the section with all possible variations to this itinerary so that you can adjust it to your own needs/wants.

As you can see from the itinerary checklist -- depending on the activities, tours, and type of accommodation you choose -- the average cost will be anywhere from 4,500 to 8,500 Australian dollars. Alternatively, you can go on guided tours. Please read the customization section so you can adjust this itinerary to your own needs and wants.

Itinerary Trip Legs

The Red Centre

Adelaide is where you start your Outback trip around Australia, onboard the GHAN Train. The first leg of your train journey takes you to Alice Springs.

Spend two days visiting the town and then hit the road to Uluru in the Red Center, for a four-day road trip. Here are more tips for a road trip to Uluru:

https://www.rockytravel.net/blog/tips-for-visiting-uluru/

The GHAN Train takes you on your next 24-hour train journey from Alice Springs to Darwin. The train stops at Katherine Gorge, where you'll be able to go on a river boat tour.

Darwin

Click to view this itinerary on Google Maps:

http://bit.ly/2ygX2S8

Spend two days in Darwin and visit the **Bicentennial Park** along the Esplanade with gorgeous views of Darwin's Harbour. Learn about its history and heritage at the **Museum and Art Gallery**.

If you're visiting from May to October, you'll be able to see Australia's most famous market the Mindl Beach Sunset Markets.
Hire a bike and go on a ride through the Marina, Cullen Bay and Fanny Bay to the East Point, which is Darwin's nature reserve.

Kakadu National Park

Go to Kakadu N.P. on a three-day 4WD tour that includes these parts: **A river cruise** in Kakadu's wetlands to see a wealth of native birdlife.

Nourlangie Rock and **Ubirr Rock,** which are two significant indigenous rock art sites with beautiful walks and lookouts.

Iconic Jim Jim Falls is a must (though it's only open in the winter: May-September). Gunlom and Maguk Falls in the southern part of the park are lesser known, but still truly special.

This Top End guide gives more tips on what to see in Kakadu N.P. https://www.rockytravel.net/australia-top-end/

Kununurra

From Darwin, take the Greyhound bus to **Kununurra**. This is a full-day bus journey to a small Outback town in North Western Australia, which is also the gateway to **Eastern Kimberley**.

Get a taste of the Purnululu National Park (a.k.a. Bungle Bungles) by visiting the **Mirina National Park** in Kununnurra (a.k.a the Lot City or Mini Bungle Bungles).

From **Kelly's Knob Lookout**, enjoy an Outback sunset and a gorgeous view of the town featuring Lake Kununurra and the Sleeping Buddha (a huge rock formation resembling a lying Buddha).

From the **Ord River Diversion Dam**, you can go on a river cruise up to Lake Argyle, or you can drive southeast out of town and go on a Lake Argyle cruise instead.

Go on a scenic flight to Purnululu National Park from Kununurra. You can read how to see this national park in one day here: https://www.rockytravel.net/exploring-the-eastern-kimberley/

And here you can read more about things to do in Kununurra:https://www.rockytravel.net/blog/what-to-do-in-kununurra/

Broome

From Kununurra, you'll fly to **Broome** to visit the Pearl of North Western Australia. Broome is where the Outback meets the ocean. With stunning coastal red rock formations and white sandy beaches, Broome has some of the prettiest beaches in Western Australia and is a popular winter destination for Southern Australians.

Take an 8 km morning walk from **Gantheaume Point** to visit the dinosaur's footprints, then continue on to **Cable Beach**, Broome's most famous.

Visit **Pearl Luggers** to learn about Broome's fascinating pearl history. Tour a pearl farm like **Willy Creek** for a unique hands-on experience.

Hire a car and drive 250 km to the north to see **Cape Leveque** and many other deserted beaches. You can spend 3 full days in Broome. From there you'll fly 50 minutes to Exmouth. Here a link to my Broome Guide:https://www.rockytravel.net/broome-the-pearl-of-north-western-australia/

Exmouth - the Coral Reef

Exmouth has over 10 surf beaches and is where the **Ningaloo Reef** starts. **Turquoise Beach** is a 30-minute drive on the western coast, and is a gorgeous spot for snorkeling in crystal clear water. On your way south, stop at **Cape Range National Park** and drive up to Charles Knife Canyon's highest point. From here, take the bush trail for spectacular views of the canyon. After a two-hour drive south, you'll arrive at **Coral Bay**, which is a small village and real haven for relaxing and snorkeling. Go on a **boat tour** to spot turtles, manta rays, and humpback whales (June-November). If you feel adventurous, you can go on a tour to swim with whale sharks (May-July).

View it live on Google Maps through this link: https://bit.ly/2l5QTPt

Shark Bay Region

Your next trip leg is about 300 km. On your way to Shark Bay, stop at **Carnarvon** to visit its Heritage Precinct, do the one-mile Jetty walk, and see the blow holes. Your first stop is 250km south at **Hamelin Pool Stromatolites** to see the oldest living fossils on earth. **Shell Beach** is a unique beach made of millions of tiny shells stretching over 120 km. Next up is **Monkey Mia** to see and feed wild bottlenose dolphins who visit the shore every day.

Take a self-guided walk in **Francois Peron National Park** and drive to the cliff tops of Cape Peron to spot sharks, manta rays, and more. Great indigenous tours are also offered, so you can learn about the cultural heritage of this area. **Denham** is the main town and airport that connects to Perth. In Denham, go to the Eagle Bluff boardwalk for a spectacular view of the ocean.

Customization Options

If you only have 20 days here is how I'd suggest reducing the length of your stay:

20-Day Itinerary

If you have 20 days I would suggest reducing the trip legs to a fewer destinations and shorten the length of your stay. Here are my suggestions:

- **Fly from Adelaide to the Red Centre and to Top End** Reduce your stay by one day in Darwin and in Alice Springs. This saves you four days.

- **Fly from Darwin to Broome** and skip the Eastern Kimberley segment, which will save you three days. Reduce your stay to two days in Broome.

- **Fly from Broome to Exmouth** and visit the Coral Bay area only. This will save you three days.

Extended Itinerary

If you can plan a longer time, let's say five-six weeks. Then you can extend your stay and plan additional trip segments. Here some options.

- **Plan seven days in the Top End Area** with daily trips to Darwin's surroundings, the Litchfield National Park, Katherine Gorge.

- **Plan a 10-14 day Kimberley Tour** from Darwin to Broome or Kununurra to Broome. This allows you to see all of the Kimberley. You can do this on a **guided 4WD tour,** or you can do it on your own - though a certain level of expertise with driving in remote Outback areas is required.

- **Plan two more days in Exmouth** or in Coral Bay for more snorkelling, wildlife experiences, relaxing and hiking walks in the Cape Range National Park.

- **Plan two more days in the Shark Bay area** for hiking and exploring the area.

- **Plan two more days in the Red Centre Area** to explore the Western and Eastern McDonnell Ranges or to stay in Alice Springs.

You can also consider doing this itinerary reverse: starting from Perth, going up north, and then south from Darwin to Adelaide, via Alice Springs. This is a great alternative if you are flying from Europe or the U.S., so that you can shorten your flight by 2 hours.

Transportation Options

This itinerary is set up to give you plenty of freedom as you will be driving by yourself, but it also includes tours and train journeys to maximize time and money. Here are my suggestions:

- **Red Centre - Uluru**

  I would not go on a tour to Uluru; this is a place that you need to be by yourself. I highly recommend going it solo. The road trip is easy and relaxed on sealed roads.

- **Kakadu National Park**

  While you can definitely drive by yourself, to explore some areas, you will need a 4WD car/campervan. As a first time traveller, I would suggest going on a three-day tour in a small group.

- **Kununurra - Eastern Kimberley**

  You can visit the town and its immediate surroundings on your own, however to drive to Purnululu National Park, you will need 4WD car. The better option is to go a one or two-day guided tour.

- **Broome - Kimberley**

  To see all of the Kimberley I would highly suggest choosing a guided tour. The average length is from 10-14 day tour. Unless you are highly experienced driving in 4WD I wouldn't go solo. Most tours start from Kununurra to Broome or from Darwin to Broome. There are also tours starting from Broome to the Kimberley and back to Broome.

- **Exmouth to Shark Bay** This area covers 800km which you can drive by yourself. You can pick daily tours along your way like walking tours in national parks, boat tours to the fringe reef, tours to swim with the sharks, or wildlife tours to see dolphins or humpbacks. If you don't fancy driving on your own, you can opt for a guided tour from Exmouth to Monkey Mia, but most tours will cover Exmouth to Perth in seven days.

Travel Resources to Itinerary no. 4

Travel Websites Red Centre + Top End

For Ayers Rock and Red Centre download this Guide:

http://www.environment.gov.au/system/files/resources/68f2af6a-2857-442a-8477-9b6e043b66cd/files/visitoressentials.pdf

For the Red Centre of Australia you can check out this page with a detailed calender events:
https://www.discovercentralaustralia.com/events/red-centre-events-calendar

For Kakadu download this Kakadu Visitor Guide:

https://parksaustralia.gov.au/kakadu/pub/visitor-guide.pdf

Getting Around

TRAIN

If you want to experience the Australian in a unique way, you should go on a train journey across the country. Here is how to do it on board of **GHAN TRAIN**. www.greatsouthernrail.com.au

BUS

Greyhound Buses offer a good network to get around the Top End of Australia. https://www.greyhound.com.au/

SELF-DRIVE car and campervan

https://www.rockytravel.net/DriveNow
https://www.rockytravel.net/DriveNow-Campervan

FLIGHTS

For the best Deals of Domestic Flights to Ayers Rock use this link: https://www.rockytravel.net/Wotif-Flights

Accommodation Red Centre

It is very expensive to stay at Ayers Rock. If you don't book your accommodation early you may end up spending 700-1000 AUD for one night. I recommend following hotels at the Yulara City Resort (the only town where you can stay at Ayers Rock)

Outback Pioneer Hotel has good rooms at reasonable prices >>
https://booki.ng/2y4TQcb

If you don't mind sharing the Outback Pioneer Lodge is a good budget option (4 dorm share with bunk beds) https://booki.ng/2y4cktz

Kings Canyon Resort – A really good place where to stay

For Ayers Rock Accommodation you can also check out this page : https://booki.ng/2IydSwh

Accommodation in the Kakadu National Park

For Accommodation in the Kakadu N.P. check out this link:
https://booki.ng/2l2motE

For Camping check out the National Parks Official Site:
https://bit.ly/2sPPbWy

Tours of Uluru + Kakadu

For Kakadu Tour check out these tours: https://bit.ly/2y4NREg

For Uluru Tours check out this link: https://bit.ly/2Jvp8ye

Travel Sites North W.A. and Central W.A.

Kununurra Visitors Centre for the Eastern Kimberley
http://www.visitkununurra.com/

Broome Visitor site www.visitbroome.com.au

For the Coral Coast in West Austalia
https://www.australiascoralcoast.com/

The Exmouth Official Site www.exmouthwa.com.au

Getting Around Western Australia

Greyhound Buses offer a good network to get around the Top End of Australia. https://www.greyhound.com.au/

Self-Drive Car and Camper Van

https://www.rockytravel.net/DriveNow
https://www.rockytravel.net/DriveNow-Campervan

Useful Travel App

Download the Fre City 2 Go App for each city and region in Australia (works online and offline) https://apple.co/2Mk8Rdj

Navigation GPS system and interactive Map (works offline) from Hema Maps https://apple.co/2sOPrVW

For camping sites in Australia download for Free Camping App https://apple.co/2Mm0Rs5 or the free camp app https://apple.co/2sZb2Kt

Accommodation in Western Australia

Check out this page for hotels in Broome: https://booki.ng/2sYYIda

For Kununurra Hotels check out this page: https://booki.ng/2sRnLQc

Tours of Western Australia

Day-Tours of Broome (4WD tours, helicopter tours etc.)
https://www.partner.viator.com/en/10250/search/broome

Day-Tours Tours for Kununurra + Outback Adventures
https://www.partner.viator.com/en/10250/Kununurra/d22937-ttd?activities=all

Western Australia Tours https://www.partner.viator.com/en/10250/travel-tips/Western-Australia-Tours/ttd

From Rocky Travel

Outback Tours Reviews

www.rockytravel.net/blog/kimberley-australia-adventure/

www.rockytravel.net/exploring-the-eastern-kimberley/

https://www.rockytravel.net/blog/the-kakadu-national-park/

https://www.rockytravel.net/exploring-kakadu-national-park/

https://www.rockytravel.net/broome-the-pearl-of-north-western-australia/